No Hands After MIDNIGHT

Poems and prose by:
Kelani Falks-Mondragon

This is for my <u>momma</u>
>As short as her fight was for us.
>It was long for her, and full of pain.

She is the strongest woman I will ever know, though she never believed it.

3 years fighting cancer, only to have Malignant Pleural Effusion (MPE)take her life, suddenly and unexpectedly.

>I hope you feel our love
>I hope you know you're missed
>I hope you are with your family
>And they all gave you a welcoming kiss

This is my grieving; this is my hurt.

>I love you momma

And I miss you more
than words could ever say.

Intro

I wrote these poems not intending to make a book, but everyone in my family pushed me and supported me to do it, so here I am.

I'm not sure what I am doing, but I do know I love writing and I hope that this book will reach people who can relate and let them know those thoughts are normal and you are not alone in them. Other than that, I'm sorry if you've lost someone in any way shape or form. It is never easy; it never gets easier you just learn to live with it. So, there's that.

And I'm sorry if poetry isn't your thing, it wasn't my mom's either! Read it slow. A turtle's pace if you will. Digest it and do it again. Every time you read it; you see it opens doors to new meanings.

Now, here is my heart laid out on paper for you.

Morphine drips

Morphine drips
Scaly lips
White knuckled
But not from holding a grip

Awake but in a half lucid trip

Morphine drips
Eyes dull
We might as well get the shovel
Nothing is in control

Except

Morphine drips
Words flick
The fan whips
Lifeless lack of desperation
They have lessened their attempts to save "em"

So

Morphine drips
Falling like stars
Falling like rain
On broken parts

Morphine drips
Settling the pain
Dropping in veins

Morphine drips
Take you away
From moments of sane

Morphine drips
Stole your light
Day is always night

Morphine drips
A smell I won't forget
Still and yet

Morphine drips
Tattered hair
Veins of blue

Disappeared
    Morphine drips

Burn

I guess I'll just die with it
Whenever that day comes
When I don't get to see the sun
When my body feels the burn
Of everyone's last words

This heartbreak that's left
It's not so gracious

BLACK VEIL

Forever is a clever word
But flighty like a bird
It's not really meant
It's just torment
An when your sanity is present
It's like a complement
So
You wear it well
That black veil
But since time is rigorous
That's where the ghost lives

<u>Your body</u>

You know that feeling
The tethering between sleep and wake
The vulnerability of your mind
Your body
One thought can control what you see
Your dreams
Your breathing
That's life.
After the loss
After the bustle
After the intensity
You're just there
Tethering on the constant
vulnerability

Salt

A jay on the fence
It's eyes so dense
Watching and waiting for the fellow
to fly
But time keeps going by
It's tail flickers
And salt scatters in glimmers
I guess the old superstition is true
Now he can't move

You

It feels like inflammation
all the noise coming into my ears
Pounding and changing how I feel
I see the lights glowing
A softer glow then years before
It's not as comforting
It's not as magical
It's missing
Missing something
And I know what it is
Does everyone else

Wrinkles

Those wrinkles on your skin
Hold stories within
I wish I could read them
All the smiles you've held
It's a deepest secret of tales

And I only got what you provided
I'm here
Waiting
You're invited

Book Frames

If words were water
I'd be drowning
But now I'm counting
To a number that makes no sense
I've lost all common sense
Out the window it flew
When I realized I couldn't keep you
A memory isn't the same
You're too far
It's to ingrained
I've gone insane
In a still frame
Locked in books
These pages are like crooks

Winter Cold

What is it about a tree in winter
It's so beautiful
It's raw and exposed
Dancing in the brisk wind
Holding onto the snow
Does it grieve its leaves?
Is it cold?
Does it just breathe and let go?

Gold plated Armour

Nothing is as happy as it was
Sometimes it feels like this sadness
might combust
With gold plated armour
I hold it in
But it's melting and getting thin
So much for any kind of protection
It's building up like some kind of
infection
But the sad
Is as it ever was

Except it's not…

It moves too fast
Too hot
And
It's a lot
So with the lies I tell myself
I'll stack them upon this shelf
Waiting for it to break

There's only so much it can take

White Flowers

It's not all sad
Sometimes I still see the colors
If I stop
I can hear the birds
But then
The hollowing illusion of happiness
filters in
Little by little
I push back
I see your smile
I see the butterflies on the white
flowers
Outside of the brick and mortar that is
holding you safe
Until we can
I hear it
I hear the beauty

<u>Wary and worn</u>

Clouds hang in the southwest sky
Presumptuous winter flakes fall in my eyes
It's cold
To the bone
The depth holds me down like stones
Wary and worn
I press on through this disdain
And somehow
The strength comes from within the pain

Waning crescent

A bird house
A nest
The comfort of the mother's chest
Hiding away from the rest
Is safety at its best
Waning crescent in the sky
How time has flown by
Holding on tight
To easier times
Still that waning crescent is up high
I take a photo
But the bird has flown by
I guess…
I'll let the moon take the lead this time

Death Queen

No words can express the feeling
When the movement of the chest
stops
The breathing
Rising up and falling down
The sound
Like a flower in its first frost
It delicately dissolves
To a place we don't know
But assume it goes
Dark or white
Somewhere out of sight
Still heavy it weighs
Drudging on in amber rays
Lightness is not a thing
When death is queen

<u>Vicious</u>

Pain for pain

    Desperate to replace it
    The emotional pain, that is
So I forage
    I test bounds
I inflict physical pain
But in reality… It's all temporary
It's all too encompassing you cannot escape it
    YOU must ENDURE it
        Soak in it… only then
    Will the weight lift… again
    Only temporarily

VICIOUS CYCLES

Twenty twenty three

It was almost the death of me
Somehow
We are hours away from 2024
I lost my bravery when I walked out
that door
Scattered water from the sky
All I could do was cry
I don't want to leave '23
you are not with me
The sound of 2024 stings
because all I have of you is what
lingers with me

<u>Turpentine</u>

Emotions burn like turpentine
Even in the sunrise
Sheets covered in streams
My breathing is louder than it seems
Her smell lingers here
Her watch
Her thoughts
And her things
My minds like a padded room
You can't hear it screams
Are you ready for this?
You say
As we wake in dismay

Tectonic

Tectonic shifts within the air
Leaves fall
It's no longer summer here
Temporary warmth covering us
All my feelings want to do is fuss
Apprehensive smiles here
And there
Are they even aware
Faces portray what words do not
I'm aching to drown in this pot

Tapestry and a thorn

If this plaster could talk
What stories would it divulge
Darkness
Death
The unknowns
All the people who didn't have their ducks in a row
All the people who've turned to stone
Whether it's the string or multiple machines
Keeping the loom
Seems every story has appending doom
The tapestry is torn
And you can't fix it with a thorn

Suicide

Last night was tough
Contemplated suicide way too much
Thoughts go running like it's a race
Not even at a steady pace
Back and forth
I know it's wrong
But I'm paralyzed
And I can't move on
Daylight breaks
Happy comes in
Before my mind starts racing again

Knowledge Overgrowing

September was the beginning of the end
When life was no longer a friend
When nothing could mend the broken parts
Everything just enhanced the dark
To come
Like a feverish dream
It feels so obscene
Knowledge overgrowing
Some things I'd be better off not knowing
Fuck it
Toss in the towel
Let it be known
My life is over now

Streetlights

Hazy streetlights
Intertwined past lives
Staying up way to late
Just for old time's sake
Never said a solution was in sight
Mediating my feelings
I rein them in tight

Storms in my eyes

The storms in my eyes could capsize
The water in my lungs could minimize
If only I could inhale
I cannot bear this load
I cannot atone
Where have you gone
I ask my soul
Lost
So weary is my mind
Burdened is my heart
It's been this way since our forced restart

Simulation madness

Where am I
I'm lost inside
The madness of a simulation
Claiming to be my day and night
Mimicking my life
With such strife
But that's not me
That's not who I used to be
I'm a torn-out page of liberation
I'm stuck in a state of sedation
The only way out is burning the page
But I can't
It's locked in a cage
With a lock I cannot pick
They took the skeleton key and gave it a nick
Nobody's able to get in
It just keeps tallying
Mark after mark
Line after line
I'm still lost in these manufactured lies

<u>Stone bones</u>

All these things I thought I wanted
I don't anymore
Feels like so many promises are just
tattered on the floor
Nothing was set in stone
But my hopes were on top
When reality hits
I'm frozen just gazing at that clock
The secondhand drops
The sound of the desperation is
ungodly loud
My soul is like stone
Cold and alone
It is weighing down my bones

<u>Tangible Throws</u>

Where did the heat go
I'm consistently cold
I'm wrapped up with tangible throws
Only to realize
They all have holes
And the unwelcoming air is splitting my bones
Lacking the compassion I've once known

<u>Smoke rings</u>

Smoke rings
whiskey and beer
Tragic that it still doesn't stop the tears
Devastating source of magic
Maybe we should switch to a new tactic
Maybe the results would be more captive
And
Maybe the loss of direction
Was a little blinding
I don't know I'm still deciding
Wherever it went
I hope we can find it
But these dark shadows keep hiding it
I hope one day it will catch our attention
Undivided

Revolution

Draped in the darkness
Just contending with the light
Never would have imagined minimal exposure would be alright
Every revolution amid my heart and mind
Has just left me in a bind
Composing lines
Rattling lies
Searching for the words
I'm fine

I'm fine…

Pendent

The moon
on my
neck
Dangling
with
another
pendent
Scribed
with
words
baring
love
Some of
which I
never got
enough
The inside that your outer held
A little tarnished but still part of a tale
Dedicated to the time
A silver necklace that will be
Forever mine

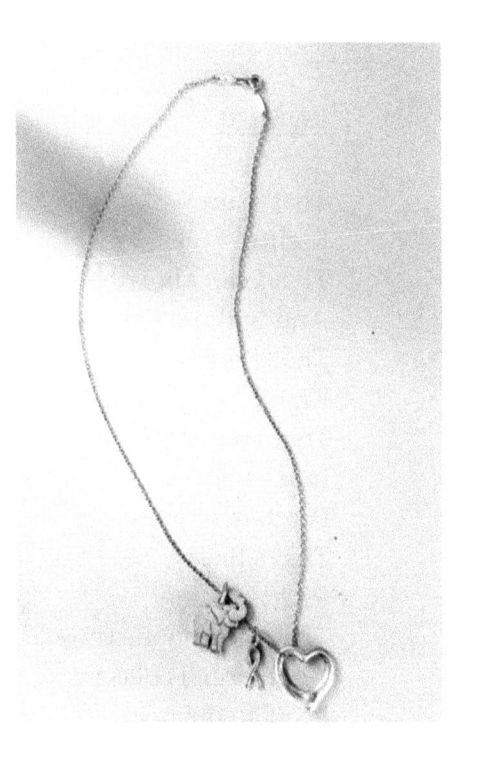

<u>Right…?</u>

That's fine
Right?
That I can't breathe
And without you sleep is obscene
That's fine
Right?
That your stuff stays
In it's now
Permanent place
That's fine
Right?
That your phone rings
Another bill collector
Adds to the pain
That's fine though
Right?
That I cry
From such a devastating goodbye
That's fine though
Right?
That my house lost the scent of you

Throughout
But that's fine
Right?
Because grief is in stages
I should be flipping through pages
and pages
So I'm fine
Right?
"You've passed those stages"
And that's fine
Right?
So I'm fine…though…

Right?

One by one

Your eyes are on him
Your face is on me
Your laughter proliferates down in my being
Petals from the roses I cut
Trickle one by one
Words of wisdom come from dads' tongue
Days go and days come
Slowly but surely

One…by…one…

Serotonin

It's late at night
And I'm in my bed
I can feel my heartbeat
And hear it in my head
Endorphins are slowing
Emotions are tip toeing
There you are in the window
Lingering like you're stuck in innuendos
But there's a problem with my serotonin
Now coming like a flood of preconceived notions

<u>Photosynthesis</u>

It's midnight
It's dark
I've lost my hands
I can't see where they are
The clouds have now uncovered the sky
And I'm standing in moon beams of white
Upon my skin
Chills compile
As I walk for miles and miles
I see my hands
Wondering around as I shiver and shake them out
Now right before sunrise
I gather thoughts behind my eyes
Now if only I could say them
But I try and words don't come out
Silence fills the air
As I gasp for a zephyr
To come and take my words
Fill my lungs I know it's what I deserve

Leaves crumble beneath my feet
I want to fall to my defeat
But lightly I step
Without any prep
Now I still don't feel alive
And the sun burns my eyes

I'm not a plant
I can't photosynthesize

Olfactory

Foreign words fall from my lips
Abbreviating words I thought weren't on my list
But here we are standing
Waiting for the next condolences
The smell is quite sweet
In this building that isn't made for the meek
I guess it's just prepared death
making my olfactory peak

Oblivion

I'm drunk
It's not what you think
Tangled in this oblivion I have
weaved
Hallucinations creep
Under these toxic words I have on
repeat
I'd kill myself
If I didn't see
All the good you have left here for me

Navigation

My compass has lost direction
Or the needle is oppressing
It's a winding path I'm trekking
But I'm chalking it up to guessing
Navigation isn't my strong suit
It's completely gone since I've lost you
Everything looks the same
Green after green
Grain after grain
Walking is getting tougher
Trudging along this lackluster

Naivety

Naivety is dripping into my palms
How am I supposed to remain calm
To touch you is cold
To see you
To see you…
Is too pigeonholed
Wires rings and multiple other things
Stop talking
To them I wish to scream
But the chattering is so overwhelming
So I fall to my knees
Hoping to stop scrambling to breathe
Grey and white tiles kaleidoscope on
the ground
As we proceed
To leave
That red and yellow gown

Bag of Tricks

Tears of pain
Tears of sorrow
Tears because there may not be tomorrow
Tears of joy
But…less and coy
Tears of stress
Tears of fear
Tears because you lost years
Tears like wax around candle wicks
Because they held you like a bag of tricks
Now
Tears are hollow
Tears of blue
Tears of agony
Because I no longer have you

My dad

Sitting in silence and absent stares
Keeping the chaos at bay
Before my brain takes its shares
Battered blunted and used
Clearly you are my muse
It's a game of tag
And today I'm it
I don't want to play anymore
I quit
Desperately clinging to what I had
I'm forever indebted
Because you left me my dad

Mile Marker 207

A decorated cross on the side of the road
You are not
It doesn't make it less tragic
Mile marker 207
Loss is loss
Whether expected or violent
Hospital room 702
Cancer
Oxygen machine
Suffocation from fighting lungs
Dead
Both dead
Gone
Missing
Lives completely incomplete
Fear
brings sleep
cold corpse

A midnight library

A midnight library I can rifle through
That's what I call the flashbacks
Unwelcoming and strangling at most
Less prevalent
Still burning a hole slowly and
painfully
Are you safe?
Because I'm not
I'm a danger in my own thoughts
It's not a safe haven like you were
It's a battlefield and I'm getting scorn
Part of me wants to vanish
Part of me wants to fight
But every part of what used to be you
is keeping me alive

Linger

The smell of the air
It's quite dense from the mountain tears
We wait and we linger here
Unaware of the beauty within

Seeking only what we see fit
Wait…stop…. breathe
There's magic within the leaves

Irresistible

      That black hole
    I could dabble in it
forever

      But I see the
sun
It's pulling me out
    It's so beautiful
Painfully beautiful

Infestation

Night has never felt like this
Like a vice
Even in the ambient light it squeezes
the air out of my lungs
How do I survive
They keep saying you are with me
and all around me
But that doesn't fucking matter
Nothing matters
It doesn't fix me
It doesn't fix this
It doesn't take away this endless ache
that only you can heal
But somehow
I am supposed to go on
So I'll float
I'll move
And I'll teeter
I'll do all I can to cleanse and cover
this wound
But I feel the infestation
I feel the rot

I feel the rip and stab and jab with every waking moment
With every sigh…
It's there

Heart strings

Strings like a web around my heart
They were holding it in place
They were the knights
Until October twenty-five
Until the swords betrayed them
Until the pain forsake them
Now here I am
Succumbing to the numb
The pain has begun

Grow old

I am homesick
For a feeling
For an empathetic stare
For a breath so sweet that is no longer here
For a connection that only a mother could spare
For a touch so meticulous
It reaches my soul
But my chance is gone it's just a hole
They took you from me
You didn't get to grow old

Flesh Coat

I'm a car with no steering wheel
I don't know what to do
Grief is a weighted stone
Pulling me down
Sinking slow
I'm without you
Wishing is more painful than reality
I feel like I'm losing vitality
The beaker has broke
It's burning my flesh coat
I feel the tears like a lump in my throat
I'm drowning…
       Quick…
              throw me a rope.

Emptiness

The epitome of abandoned
The state of losing control
Bestow upon her
While you're in a blur
Clawing and scraping to get by
With only emptiness on your side
Sensations of her upon your skin
Guiding you to start living again

Devilish Ghost

I can't shake this devilish ghost
I'm impaired
So now you think it's a joke
I promise I can prove it's there
Just give me a minute
I swear
I'm not beyond repair
Give me those pills
I'll sort it out
I'm trying to get better now

Deposition

Brown was the color of the dirt
Brown was the color of your hair
Mercurial was how we were
Until you became ill
Then all of our world was at a
standstill
Centrally significant
All our other pain became irrelevant
The deposition of this meeting is
interminable
Over a life they just consider
terminable

Cylindrical cycles

Death is a villain
Crying tears from within
Cylindrical cycles of a maddening pattern
How do you escape such a covert transgression
Maybe
It's time
So the passion for prose is effervescent
As we wait in emotional traffic
Stuck in words deeper then sand
Tossing and turning just trying to make amends

Cracks

Sadness is bleeding through the
cracks
I can't get away
It's consuming me
Suffocating me
Surrounding me
It's presumptuous

Countervailing

Puddles on the pavement
Glistening from the streetlights
Every footstep full of despite
It's so dark and the sky is wailing
My eyes are stuck countervailing
What has happened where have you gone
We turned the corner
      sadly alone
Drenched in cold
Soaked
      To the bone

Coffee

He makes his coffee
And grabs her too
Delicately he dances around room to room
At the table he sits wishing her veins were blue
Yet black burns his eyes with such a tearful yearn
To have anything except this beautiful urn

Christmas Recipe

What is it that makes it Christmas
It used to be you
YOUR Christmas ham
      So I tried
You didn't write it down Mom…
I don't know
I didn't know
I was so lost
I tried
I don't want it
It doesn't make Christmas
It lost Christmas

Now it's just ham

<u>Cake is just cake</u>

Cake is just cake
Until there's a happy before it
And the assumption of certain
emotions you should feel
But lacking the life that gave you life
will make you kneel
The distance between the floor and
you appear less
You can't bow and you can't digress

Burgundy drapes

Eyes wide open
Eyes wide shut
Can't decide which one means too much
Burgundy drapes cover the stage
With an ending
That no one craves
Caves and tunnels in my mind
With the main actress left far behind
Boards and boarders now blocking my mind
Tragedy has fallen and darkened my eyes

Bombardment

What is a fire without warmth
It's just ambient light pondering its heat
It's just lingering sorrow
Searching
Searching
With a flicker of flint
A tress of yarn
Something to spark the glimmer
Something to slow the bombardment of dejection
Searching and searching just until the yearning is fulfilled
Flames and flames of burning desperation

Ambivalent

To keep you was the idea
But into the waves you crashed
Where you were tossed
And turned
With such thrash
Ambivalent we stand
With such helpless hands
Leading a life with joyless plans
With every intention we grapple to understand
Why the world had this plan

2,000 degrees

Empathy is enraging
Unless you've heard that 2,000
degrees blazing
That sound is intimidating
Ashes and ashes along with a casket
Another white room that was
traumatic
Oval table
Chairs added
Picking and choosing how to have it

I left a note with you
Did you grab it?

Blueprint

I throw a rock at a wall
And watch it fall
Something that is blank
Can't hold anything at all
Your emotions break
As I call out
I don't mean to put your heart in a drought
I try to capture all I can
But something is broken now
If I could just understand
But sometimes blueprints get lost in a master plan

Sparrow & Butterfly

It's yellow and black
Its strange pattern brings it back
Daily it dips and dives
Fluttering ever so kind
Like the wind is on its side
It's black and yellow
Such aim like an arrow
Being watched by the sparrow
Who sits upon the lamppost so high
Waiting and watching the butterfly

Disagreeable

A cold touch on my arm
Lingers like the aftermath of a storm
The prescience makes you a little
more informed
The impression it makes may be a
little disagreeable
But the proof it leaves is believable

Assorted love

Assorted love here and there
Depictions of a time better spared
Leave behind all the despair
For an idolization of a better pair
Clowning upon you for a look
Sensational loves make the books

Sentimental Reluctance

My anger can be defiling
Though I know it's a once in a while thing
Timid actions of a consequence
Stirs up sentimental reluctance

Stairs and stairs to get nowhere
Except another morning

Spent mourning…

Bewildered

The dark is thick
And a little chronic
The light is bewildered with a
complexity I can't comprehend
I'm grasping and grasping but it has
no hands
So I just grapple with the night to no
end
Fighting
Until the dark isn't so thick again

<u>Fiend</u>

Waveless water rushing over me
Just as I it doesn't breathe
Washing and washing trying to clean
But I come to find its just a fiend
Drowning
Drowning now
Toss the chains
I'm about to bow
In parallel pain

Sutures

Skin and bones without a soul
Lying down like you're playing a role
Eyes closed and in a casket
We all see it nobody wants to ask it
Sutures hold your jaw
You don't look like your screaming
In the case like an angel
You look like you're dreaming

Loss of quarrels

Pale and cold
Where is your glow

Why is the life scattering from your eyes
I pace by and try to grab it
Piece by piece its flying faster
Panicking I turn around
It's shattered now like glass on the ground
There's no more decency for your morals
Leaving the room loss of quarrels

Fan is on
You were hot

Turned it off because now..
                        You are not

Beast

Happiness is brittle
With heavy hands we belittle
Breaking it with conviction
To overcome an insurmountable
depiction

Lastly but not least
You cannot tame the beast

Tacking

Feet on the ground
But I'm not grounded
I feel so hopeless
These thoughts are becoming ferocious
Tacking upon a lost vision
Leaving me in a head on collision
Dizzied up by the sound
My own thoughts tease me like a clown
An agonizing reality conforms my brain
While I wish for a time with no pain

Inferiority

Tears splattered
We gathered
Love holds us but it's a broken ladder
Unsteady now
We stumble
It really makes you crumble
Inferiority takes precedence
Taking all the evidence

Hippocampus

Joy is inadequate
My hippocampus is on the battlefront
Keeping on keeping
Manifesting daily
It's not working
I'm rationalizing lately
Tossing and turning
It's a fleeting sight
To wake up crying in the density of twilight

Thieving

Captivating and tonic
Filled with ideals less than iconic
Return for misery
Thieving with trickery
Tempting the ghost
Providing the most

Jocund

Coffee is hot
The magnetic pull from this moon is nonstop
Hoping for a sliver of jocund
To pierce
To puncture
To enter
This cavern
That holds my brain
But like a recluse
It holds nothing of use
Though it thinks it has it all
Impenetrable darkness is a downfall
While I stare at coffee ring stains
I finally let it enter
Without strain

Scratches

Wood floors
Dark
Adorned with scratches
Made by the beauty of life's patches
She hated the walls
He hung the installs
Frame upon frame
Each by name
A magnificent home the house
became

Mysterious

Morning is beautiful
Mourning is delicate
Tiptoeing around all the elements
Leaving a mysterious mark
Suddenly afraid of the dark
Calmly approaching something cynical
Forced to make it typical
Laying flat on your back
Hoping that's the last whack

Analyzing Eyes

Ferociously meeting myself in the mirror
Confused there must have been an error
I don't remember it like this
I'm watching me
Looking for you
But I'm left standing without a clue
I'm stuck staring at my face
Analyzing eyes find everything I hate
These visual facades are heathens
When do I hit the age of reason
Because I can't take this no more
And it's worse than before
Since you left
It's all too much weight on my chest
But whatever
It's just
When you were here
It was the best

FUCK

Fuck

I need you

Metaphorically heavy

Pressed you into parting stones
Now you go where I go
Is it your brain
Is it your heart
I ponder as I crave a restart
The white feels so pure
To love it is obscure
Metaphorically heavy
Holding it to see you like I haven't already

<u>Stay STAY stay</u>

Alone I wait
Cold and out of place
Come and save me
I whisper loss of words as I long for
your embrace
Turn your cardinal around
You're going the wrong
way
The path
It's led you astray
I'm here and the light is
beginning to fade
I'm here
Please
I beg you
Come back to stay

Lobotomy

Give me a lobotomy
So these memories don't consume me
Looming around like some kind of aura
What do you do when they destroy ya
Strangling hand around my throat
Taking my last chance of hope

But its just me

Lithium

I'm a human receptacle for all things
that are unmeasurable
And so I feel like lithium
The pill form
Swallowed in
Where I'm going from where I began
I'm here there's no end
Dumping and dumping
Now I'm full
Feeling like a fool
Left
Alone
With no one to come and empty you
Self-pity becomes your life
Coming at me like a device
Limited conditions
Trash can edition

<u>Vomit</u>

The thought of you tempts me to vomit
But that's not the way I want it
It's the constant reminder of what happened
Causing the good memories to dampen
Soaking wet and crumbling apart
Leaving me battered in the dark
Anticipating the lift
For the world to shift

Hawthorn

Safety is swept underneath
On the ground we sit and sleep
Once the coast is clear
We can then reappear
The hawthorn is valid
So we listen to its ballad
Until it goes quiet
Then we start the riot

A little thing

I walk with my dad into your room.
It was cold and you were there with
your legs out because you were hot.
I walked up to you and said hi and
my lips met your forehead.
Your eyes weren't there but your
brain partly was.
You said "hi baby", yet I still question
if you knew I was there.

In person.

You are so tired; you fight to breathe.
Tossing your head around to fight the
sleep.
The door opens and they come in to
give you medicine once again.
Dad must grab some papers from
another doctor,
You panic like he forgot ya.
Your head is pounding now, you're
calling the nurses out loud.

"Oh god" you say because your head is hurting and it's not like the other days.
I'm holding your hand saying hang on Momma, the nurses are coming in for ya.
If you could cry, I know there'd, be a river, but you haven't drank, there's no fluid in ya.
Dad is back and I tell him the news. He says he knows and again the nurses greet you.
We are hungry so we say "I love you". Grab some chick-fil-a and reappear.
Eating and smiling because we are all near.
We look at you, as you muster up and say "pear"
Confused dad says what was that babe?
It's like you are calling to his grave.
We settle in for the night.
Didn't know that was our last goodbye.

Kerosene

Douse me in kerosene
Maybe I'll go back to being pristine
Letting you down with certain habits
I don't have you
So I grab it
Maybe it'll cleanse
Maybe it'll clean
Until then I'll keep breaking
Hoping to find the old me in the making

New Shoes

Kids got new shoes today
All I could think about was what you would say
How you would call and say they were so tall
And have them test them out down the hall
Running and jumping while you cheered them on
Laughing saying you love them until dawn
But now you rest
In perfect peace
It's like you're here
But not personally

Cannon Ball

A cannon ball flew in
Knocking out what was once fit in
I don't know what I expected
Just thought
Maybe it would be deflected
By all the useful words of concern
But there's something I learned
On the brink of seizing
The malice is keeping
And here I am
Played a fool
I thought they were true
The intentions you set
Now I feel full of regret
For thinking they consistently cared
No
My emotions can't be spared

Paradoxical

Feeling paradoxical
Letting on of what is subtropical
Contaminating my brain with all this rain
Let a cyclone in and it brings a collection of pain
I enjoy the happy
But grab the sad
The conflicting of emotions is what makes me mad

<u>Melancholy</u>

Yellow grass and blue skies
Somewhere in between
There are eyes
Searching for reconciliation
But finding only frustration
Deprivation
And starvation
How do you permeate a notion
When you lack devotion
Like…where are you even going
I'm so full of self loathing
So much so
I'm gloating

Pathetically melancholy

Radiating

What are these pictures up for
Sometimes I want to put them in a drawer
I feel an insatiable ache as I glance
Then I'm stuck in a trance
If I just take them down
Maybe I won't have a meltdown
But I need them up
The warmth radiating fills my cup

You didn't

Your blue eyes didn't get to see the sunrise
Your skin didn't get to feel the ray from the autumn sun
Your ears didn't get to hear us say I love you as the day begun
You didn't get to go home
You didn't get to roam
You didn't get to hug us
We didn't get to discuss
We didn't get to ask
We didn't get to laugh
You didn't get peace
You didn't get to increase
You didn't get to cry

YOU DIDN'T GET TO SAY GOODBYE

You didn't
We didn't

YOU DIDN'T

Cataclysm

Scaling the cliffs as the water departed
So much is uncharted
Gravity is pulling me down
Now I'm fighting against the ground
The cataclysm of demise
Now you live in disguise
Turmoil has struck
And left you

Fucked up

Plateau

I thought that I missed the place
where you were happy
Turns out I miss the place where I last
had you
You live and you learn I guess
The pattern is just free hand
Everything is the same here
Except
The floors will never carry you
The walls will never hear you
And the roof just hangs
And I have hunger pangs
Lasting and endless
It's horrendous
It isn't fair
Food feels like air
Forced but necessary for life
But still have the hunger pangs as
described
Beginning to think it's not what I
thought
My insides just keeping up the assault
Is it heartbreak

And hunger pangs were a mistake
If that is so
Please
Please
Please
Let me know when it plateaus

Eulogy

Walking amongst the clouds
What would happen if you fell down
Appear in our presence
Leave an undoubtable essence
So I'm struggling to adjust
I'm about to combust
Because I've been screaming
And I'm angry
And nothing here can save me
So I just reread your eulogy
In disbelief
On repeat

Iridescent glow

The sun is illuminating the window
Giving off an iridescent glow
But the shadows dance around the
glass in dysphoria
Ransacking all the euphoria
Leaving me bound to sorrow
And I've run out of happy to borrow
So this evening my tears will patter
Maybe tomorrow
Things will actually matter
I can't define how I will become right
Just know that it won't be tonight

Holy Water

The holy water burns
It's like the dark shadows are trying
to make me conform
They are beckoning
It's a swarm
Help me
I'm in dismay
I'm scared
I tried to pray
It feels useless I'm tantalizing to them
I can't get out I'm stuck in this
bullpen
So I freeze and close my eyes wishing
them gone
Squeezing them tight
So I can move on

Intoxicated

I miss the clink of ice
Falling in your wine glass
With rosy cheeks you'd laugh
But I wish I could make you mad at me
I wish you'd make me roll my eyes
Be frustrated at your threats of late-night goodbyes
Yelling and fighting
Just to feel alive
Minutes take hours to get by
Understandings misunderstood
By me and you
But even the end wasn't complicated
You were intoxicated
All you wanted was comfort
But the words always came first
The hurt
Was strangling and left us dangling
In a dangerous spot
Full of unlucky thoughts
Your protection was not needed
We weren't the ones bleeding

Black blazer

The clouds hang in the sky
Just like that night
Your black blazer
The drive
The dog who also didn't know it was the end of its life
Sadness pouring down
All around
No escape
Emotionlessly bound
In a constant state of nausea

Today is just an eerie reminder of the night we lost her

<u>Opal</u>

I wish I could find the door
That would lead me to the portal
Is it white
Is it opal
Just need to find my bearings
Then maybe I could start caring
How do I get to where you are
Without taking it too far
Everything to feel you
Has opened doors to another world
It's frightening
Can you safeguard me, curled
I'll stop feeling infected
When I feel protected

<u>What degree</u>

You were here
The next day gone
I still can't process that in my dome
Don't understand why you didn't
come home
In all fairness
I didn't know
I didn't know you were gonna go
They never told us what they knew
They had a whole fuckin crew
We just sat there waiting constantly
debating
Are we where we should be
How bad is it
To what degree
But nobody told us

So we had no time
To discuss

Coated blanket of wool

Steam off the road
Evaporates into the cold with no where to go
Is that like the soul?
Every step I take the earth crumbles under my feet
Isn't life kind of neat
A coated blanket of wool
Covering me while I feel so pitiful
Bargaining with the sky to stop the chilly supply
My trajectory is aiming too high
Standing amongst the weeds
Arms reached
SCREAMING
      When will I have peace

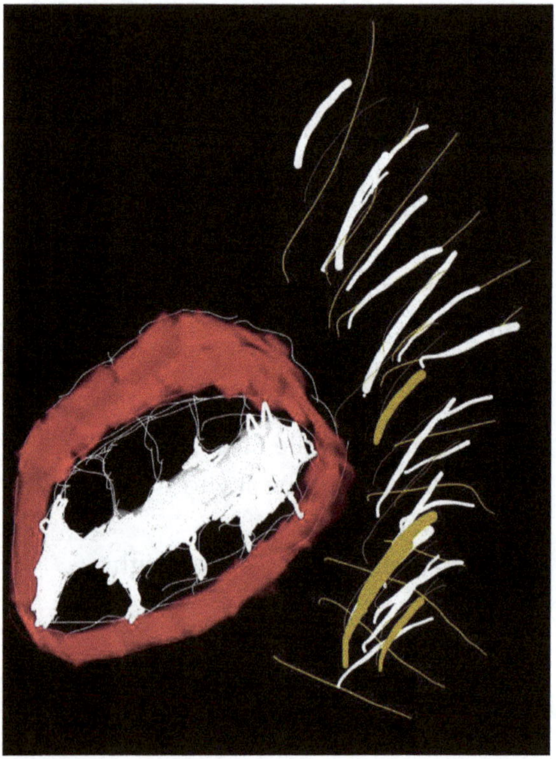

Dross

The reason I don't say what I feel when I speak
It has a lingering effect that isn't for the weak
My feet have abandoned the ground
The depth of my pain is profound
My reluctance to reveal details of my loss
Is to save you from the heavy dross

Ivy

Sad eyes staring in the mirror
Wondering if they will ever become clearer
Day by day they are just the same
A consequence of this pain
Embedding upon me like ivy
Leaving marks like a secret diary

<u>Vanity and sanity</u>

A ship cutting through the ocean waves
A tide full of rip currents pulling everything away
My sanity
My vanity
It's taken it all away
I have nothing left to display
I can't get it back
Unless you throw me some slack
Come…please…give me a raft

Crestfallen

Never thought this day would come
Where I didn't have a mom
But it's here and now I'm alive
living cold and numb
It affects you in a way
That you cannot illustrate
And life has you in a checkmate
A telltale of lies
And some manipulation of my eyes
Somehow presses me to survive
Doused and crestfallen
Emotionally in need of a solen

Bilious

Walking on a tight rope
Alone
Missed my step an inch east
I hope there is a net so I don't fall to
my defeat
Missing you is a constant state of
falling
Bilious and befuddled
One look at me you see I'm troubled

Envy

Patterns of the happy I used to have
Got taken away and cut into halves
Envy is the epitome of my covetousness
Leaving me endowed in my inculpableness
Losing you has bruised me blue
All I can do is disassociate without you

Innuendos

The plasters painted with innuendos
My shirt
Splattered with your words
Between what's underneath and
what's unheard
We're all lost and absurd
You've turned around
Still they took you down
It's not the rug
But the ground that keeps you
They took it all
Just to leave you

Abyss

My head is an empty void
I run to the ends trying to find you
I can't remember your voice
Where are you?
I'm drowning in all this other noise
Please come back
It's not fair
I can't stand to see that empty chair
How am I supposed to do this
I am so sorry I couldn't save you from the abyss
Now a ton of bricks weigh on my chest
And they just won't lift
No matter how hard I protest

Hiraeth

The hiraeth I have to be
metaphorically in your heart where I
used too
Since the day that ache has
treacherously grew
Unbeknownst to me
It became hard to see
And bad things come in threes
One slippery slope
Without a rope
Gone
Like the last of my hope

Plays

I lay here unscathed
Thinking of past plays
They rerun in my head like some kind
of mental set stage
As I return back to my brain
My head pounds in pain

<u>See you again</u>

It just hit me like a fuckin ton of bricks….

I never get to see you again….

Torture of love

This sunshine doesn't feel the same
It almost feels like rain
I guess that's because my heart is
forever in pain

Your memory isn't enough for me

Some days
I wish they would just let me fuckin
be
But here they come again
Just forcing me to contemplate
It's like I just want it to end
But it's the torture of love mixed with
nothing left to befriend
And I keep rememberin'

Repercussions

Repercussions from the silence on the
other end of the phone burns
Little do you know….
I still wait

I'll always wait….

Good points

It's a hostage situation
It doesn't matter what points I'm makin'
In my own mind
I've capsized…

Clocks

I had a dream
I watched you die over and over
It felt real
Back in September when you were alive
You had a dream you watched you dad die
Over and over
It felt real
In my house
It's haunted
All of it
Corner to corner
I feel like a performer
Living in a box
With too many clocks
Where the hurt never stops
Like the hands…. On the clocks

Death

She didn't even get to enjoy morning coffee anymore

And it was her favorite thing

Somber

Tears puddled on my nose bridge
Some running down my cheek
As I lay here in silence
My emotions speak
I can't get a grip on reality
It's way to slippery
So I just bathe in my somber
In lackluster dishonor

Mom

Have you ever gone to sleep
Then woke up and didn't have a mom
anymore?

Because I have…

Strangling

Looking at you through my hands
Grimacing as I stand
The monster in my head
Takes command
Fuck it
I have nothing left to lose
My fist are already bruised
Hands tied
It's like a noose

Everest

Paperclip head man
In my brain
Running around
Has no hands no feet
What does it mean
Everything was so clean
Have I lost it all
Maybe I should just move to Nepal
And climb to the peak
Where the atmospheric pressure
Will just squeeze the life out of me

Bloodhound

Flimsy hands
Holding onto memories as they flow like sand
Where are they going as they fall
How come they don't come when I call
Like a bloodhound I try to track them down
All I find is a nervous breakdown

Why can't you

WHY CAN'T YOU

Why can't you just come back
Without you I see all black
And still the hands of time
Never turn back

Puppet

I'm a puppet in a puppet master game
I'm walking through a fireless flame
Where are you I say
As I call out your name
No answer brings endless pain
Convert this silence to laughter
So we can just have our happy ever after

Vital fluid

An empty vessel of a heart
With a thorny garden pulling it apart
Stabbing and piercing
I'm not sure where to stand
There's blood dripping from my hands
I can't grasp it
It's slipping
How can I save me
When you are the one I am craving
But I can't have you
Your vital fluid no longer runs through
An empty shell
Turned to dust
Now we have to…. Adjust

To make thigs feel

This is the part where we turn to ash
This is the part where dreams clash
So now is the part where everything changes

We are all on separate pages

What we've relied on has vanished

Because of the many things we couldn't manage

Precedented

Odd and uncomfortable
To have me around
Unless you're there with me
When I come down
Precedented actions confirm my
conflictions
With the lack of you
I could use prescriptions
Yet here I am standing
Not tall
On the brink and destine to fall
Don't make me feel shameful for
crying
It wasn't your heart dying

Bottle rot

How sad it is to be me
I gather endless amounts of sympathy
Except for the ones who have
forgotten
They've left that thought in a bottle
Rottin'
Going on about their day
But here I am pacing in the pain
Day in and day out
I'm waiting for happiness to come out
Like a word on the tip of my tongue
I can't remember because of the numb
A sacred place I cannot find
It's like it's calcified in my mind
So I lay here awake
When I should sleep
With happy thoughts
That just feel cheap

RUG

I wasted five hours contemplating
And things got to aggravating
But somehow…now…
It matters too much
That this house doesn't feel like home
I don't know what to do
Or where to go
It's surface level regret
But it's seeping through like butter on a baguette
Realizing I can't go back
To the house that was a fast track
To see you
To hold you
To undo
But the traveled road grew old
The cracks became craters
Left to the curators
But those cracks bore into me
It's not a memory but a piece
Santa rosa
Fort Sumner
Melrose

Clovis
All for you and I hope you know this
And I hate that
We had to go
An unfortunate tour
Just to lose
Something so pure

Metamorphic

If there was a story I could write
It would be how you put up a fight
Till your lungs collapsed
And your heart stopped
You were always a metamorphic rock
Tough as nails
Able to open all our shells
So if you wonder if you are missed
If you look now
We are all in a crisis

Late night

The thirst for interactions I cannot have
It carries a lot of weight like a cement bag
It's not just you I miss
It's everything that comes with your presence
Late night watching tv
With our laughter that was lengthy
In a big world my loss is one of many
But you were my world and that is heavy

Elephant

Sure it's fine
I'll hold it together
I know
I look like I'm falling apart
Because… well fuck…
I'm surviving off a broken heart

But sure it's fine
I'll smile and laugh
Like I have every half
But fuck
I'm broken apart

And sure I'm fine
We are all together
It's never been better
But fuck
Acknowledge the elephant in the room
We are not together
It's missing her too

Sure it's fine

They assume the pain is less then
It was the day it happened

But

Fuck you
For not asking
Call it what it is
I will forgive
But I just want to understand why
Firsthand

Dreamland

To feel your embrace
Was a sense of grace
In a dream land
You held my hand
It was so brief
But it was a sense of relief
I will ache for you forever
I don't know where you are
But I hope that you are better

So much love I have for you
I just wish my dreams were true

Chump

Jokes on me
I lost what I never thought I would
It took everything it could
Left me here like a chump
With my throat in a lump
Twisting the knife
In spite
I guess that's life

Flinch

I watched day turn to dark
All with a lasting broken heart
Now it's dragging on
Like the memories of the hospital bed
you were on
The weight of it all is immense
And it makes me flinch
How unfair I have to carry this
around
It's way to profound
You shouldn't have left
You should still have your breath
I beg you to come back
Even though I know
It don't work like that

Stained

People's voices in my mind clutter
Running down dripping out my ears
like they're gutters
Caring or inflating their own ego
Again
Here we go
Words of wisdom they claim
As I feel the dwindling flame
Taking
Taking
Taking…. up my time
It almost feels like a crime
Because yet again
I am stained
As I had no time to explain

Traffic

Insincerity harboring in you
I'm not sure of what to do
Traffic pounding in my eyes
Convincing me with your lies
I can't diverge
It's a broken path
It's like all I feel are laughs
Inside its deep
This sorrow on repeat
But there you are
In your peace

Voice

I have to talk about you in the past tense
And if feels all too much like a penance
I just can't gather it all up
The past, present and future
They are holding me down like a suture
Trying to move forward
But my ears just want to hear your words
Say it
Just say it
But you can't
You've lost your voice
And your mouth

Caves carved

Riverbeds
Train tracks
What used to be full
Isn't
Droughts drawn out too long
Seems the world is wrong
The main veins lead astray
Gives us what we have today
A fucked-up place
Disappointment at a steady pace
Empty caves carved into my mind
It took it all and left me in a bind
Where you used to stand
Is empty and I just can't understand
But what used to be
Is never a guarantee

Mantel

You don't have a grave
You are free
You are tethered to me
But still you're trapped lifelessly
surrounded in black
Do I keep this close so it's you I never
lack
Is this how you wanted to be
Or is it what we wanted to see
If preparation was taken
Maybe I wouldn't feel mistaken

And there you sit
On the beautiful mantel
Substantial

Ceasefire

Words flying like bullets
Looks dropping like bombs
It's like a war zone
Everything is getting blown
Where do I go
Where do I run
They are bringing in the brigade
It feels like a grenade
I'm scattered to pieces
Because of the deceases

Ceasefire
I don't have what you require
It's the end
Let's not pretend

Lightless

Laying in my bed
I have a place for my head
Holding the blanket that kept you
warm
It's white pink and orange
Some tassels on the end are braided
I know it was you and it left me jaded
Thoughts run rabid in my brain
I wish they could be detained
But here we are

You're still lifeless
And my eyes
My eyes

They are lightless

Tattoo

Semicolon with wings
a butterfly it seems
Forever on your wrist

Should you exist

Taken along with you
Something you can't undo
Found now upon my arm
I'm wearing it like a charm
It's flying flower
To flower
Something that will forever be
Ours

Hemlock prison

I do my best work tired
Maybe because I have nothing left to aspire to
So dungeons don't seem bad
Take me in and toss me like a rag
Slam the iron
And feed me bread
It's okay
I already feel dead
Inside
Leave a stem of hemlock
On the block
Me and it need to talk
It's cold and late
And the ground is wet
I see somebody I haven't met
Turning corners
Doing rounds
White flowers are glowing now
It's not as bad as it seems
My subconscious is saying to me
A wretched prisoner in a prison
I wish to be living the life I'm missing

But gates of iron lock me in
And I see the beginning of the end

Wind chimes

Wind chimes singing in the breeze
It's pretty but it takes much more to appease
Now that you've left
Taking my simple joys I possessed
It's a struggle daily
It affected me greatly

Loud house

It can be a beautiful thing
When it takes the person filled with insurmountable pain
But the others remain
Now we are surviving while you lay lame
Can you see what we've became
Tarnished blacked and bruised
Just feeling emotionally used
And this house is loud
But it doesn't speak
It's the walls and floors
That make me feel weak

Tenterhooks

Their dirty shoes have walked on my heart
Left an imprint of something dark
Tangled up all my mind
But it's the life I've been assigned
Gathered up like a bunch of books
Holding me like tenterhooks
Stretched and it's unfair
All because what's broke is beyond repair

MAN

The sleeplessness is worse
Then the shadow man who looms
over me as I rest
Awoken with a heaviness on my chest
If I could get these words to convey
my thoughts
Maybe I wouldn't be so distraught
Maybe
Maybe
I could escape all this darkness that
proceeds to come my way
Just run and run
But the shadow man stays

<u>I love you</u>

Love you
I do love you
More than you knew
It's all past tense now and it unfairly flew
The sweet smell when you gave me a hug
You made sure you held me so snug
I wish I had taken more pictures in my mind
But I didn't know I was going to have to leave you behind
Your soul evaporated from this earth
Leaving me struggling with self-worth

Not tonight

A waterfall of words falling from my eyes
Just trickling down covering my thighs

I'll be okay…
.
.
.
.
.
Just not tonight

Cyanide bowl

Slowly but surely I think I feel them dissolving
But the feelings keep revolving
Like an upset pattern of fear
Puddling like cyanide tears
Into a bowl they sit
Waiting for me to commit
It's a fight
A tournament
And it's heavy
Dreaming it was over already
And the sky could eat it all
Every last downfall
It's not a hero but a villain
And I'm just a docile civilian
Weak willed and small
With too much pain to recall
But over there whistling with a gleam
The cyanide bowl swears to get me clean

Falling anguish

With laughter comes sadness
A combination that brings madness
Turning a corner in hopes on the other side something grabs me
Like a Skelton key
To lead me away
To open doors that take this pain
Change this frame
Fast forward through the insane
Flip this script
Why is my happiness held in a crypt
I beat it and beat it but it doesn't crack
My falling anguish has made it too
Compact

Taunt

Tranquility is having a full cup
Somehow mine got corrupt
I'm tip toeing around all the bones
Dodging all the stones
Unwittingly I've crossed the grass
Now I'm watching myself through the glass
It's like I'm haunted
Detached is the last thing I wanted
In attempting to turn over a new leaf
It was so brief

Then it was gone
Like a sick taunt

<u>All was fine</u>

Your clothes they hang
As the light scent of you fades
In the darkened closet your favorite
sweater still stays
By the mirror you kept
Your watch as you slept
Your hollowed foot steps traced a line
From the bathroom
To bed when
All
Was
Fine

Solar eclipse

As a solar eclipse takes place
The darkness feels like a heavy suitcase
People stand in herds amazed
But you called me on the last one
In your last days
In my grief-stricken silence
I wish I was eyeless
Because what was once stunning
Is just so…… unbecoming

MEDICAL

AN ABSURD AMOUNT OF PAIN

THAT'S WHAT IT'S LIKE TO LOSE
THE GAME

FATE DOESN'T STAND A CHANCE

WHEN MEDICAL INTERVENTION
LEADS THE DANCE

IT'S POP THIS
TAKE THAT

FOR THREE WEEKS THEN COME
BACK
side effects don't matter
JUST THE BILLS THEY GATHER

Beauty

You made the pansies grow
With such beautiful control
And the beauty from your fingers
Made all the smells linger
Looking at what you have created
Was amazing
But now that beauty has been
manipulated

Lost atoms

I know they hear it calling
They keep waiting but it's not
stopping
And I keep swearing it's not me
They find it hard to believe
The pear of anguish is moving in
But it's not me
I haven't sinned
It's the mimic calling from room ten
I'm lost in a maze of matters
And at this point I'm just atoms
Wasting your space
They're calling me a basket case
Turn the lights on I swear it's not me
But the hall is completely empty
There's no rooms
No doors
That just leaves myself
I must ignore

Happiness

There is still happiness
There is still amazement
You just have to try harder to hold
onto it
It's all there
Like it was
Also
Like it wasn't

It's beautifully tragic

<u>Emotional overthrow</u>

I wonder how many other people are going on about their day grieving
A consistent one
Has it been years…months…weeks…days
If I could read their hearts I would know
But I can't
So I go on with loaded questions in dismay
I want to ask
To relate maybe
But I don't
Because then it begs a story
A story maybe we don't want to share but feel obligated
And no one can relate
Because to each their own in an emotional overthrow
Because your life is just a tale….

And not everyone cares

Ashtray

Sometimes the sun appears afraid
Hiding behind many clouds of gray
Waiting for the sky to cry
So maybe I could be baptized
But I watch ashes fall in the ashtray so brittle
With a cigarette in hand I just belittle
And nothing wants to save me
Because I keep screaming like a banshee

Forward

When all stops… gather yourself
You're fighting to find the wealth
Move forward in a perpetual motion
You'll figure out where you are going
The pull from behind can be
overcame
Just follow the flame
Life is a word game

Don't let it confuse you
You can make it through

Just thoughts
I should follow myself

Masterpiece

My body is a vessel for your life
To keep you safe whatever should arise
Tiny little fingers and tiny little toes
I almost got to imagine you in clothes
But there was a fault in how you were planted
And I didn't know so I took you for granted
Now I sit here beckoning for peace
All because you were supposed to be a masterpiece

<u>Paper airplane</u>

As my eyes cry a story that no one can see
I wail out in misery
So I sit… and make a paper airplane
Take me back and ease my mind
I halfway whisper as I make it fly
When you weren't just a memory
You were sitting right here with me
When your skin was warm
And it wasn't a constant storm
Because I'm trying
But the missing you is amplifying

Tired

I'm exhausted
And it's holding me down like rocks in my pockets
A tragic ending to a fairytale that would be fine if you and I solved it
But here I am hands hanging down
I've been tired so long I feel like a clown
Eyes hollowed like I've been evicted

But that's just what the mirror depicted

A toll taken after what I've seen Darlin'
It takes a while to get clean

1:02 am

It's midnight, I'm alright just lying by your bedside.
You're beautiful and finally asleep.
A memory I'll keep locked inside of me.
Lights are flipped on, it's 1:02 am you're surrounded, I'm awaken by a grueling sound of concern.
"Wake up" they are saying with haste in their voice.
I'm confused, looking at you I'm in disbelief.
I turn to my left as dad slowly musters the energy to stand, I see it, I see his face drain, I see the answers in his eyes.
Now I can't breathe, he can't breathe, they won't stop talking, the questions seem to never end….

all while, you lay there, cold, still and alone.

Now, we have to go….without you, without our heart, with loss of breath. To go home, but I didn't want to go home.

I didn't want to leave you; I don't want to feel this.

But when you left your body next to me,
Where did you go?

Souvenir

Inside of my
memory
keeper
You stand forlornly like a gatekeeper
And it's like I'm outside of a snow
globe
Holding the most precious thing I've
ever known
Delicately
And mournful you look
For a reach that I've mistook
And whilst your voice runs on ferric
tape
Your portraits fall like a paper drape
Into my suffering they puddle
Turning everything into watercolor
The glass is now stained
On this souvenir left in my brain

Mosaic

My trapped tears are attempting to break free
And my whole body would agree
Sensations dangle to bate me in
Their an angler it's hurting under my skin
Pulling and pulling
Now they've reeled me in
Tragically falling and on the descend
Trying not to break
As I bend
But a mosaic is a beautiful end

Loudly quiet

The smell of hope lingers on my breath
I open the passenger door with monumental regret
With despondent breath I grab you
But it's not the way I want too
The white flowers are blooming on the trees
Last time you were here they made you sneeze
But that's okay it will all pass
Soon enough I'll be packing my bags
Feels like I'm leaving something…
To break even…?
To get something to believe in?
I'm not really sure
Maybe some kind of cure
And when the quiet gets loud
And there's no room for a crowd
Douse me with drips and flick the candle wicks
Somehow the crystal has lost its shine
I struggle to see with frosted eyes

And tears of sorrow sting my face
dripping from my chin as I'm
pleading with my brain to make its
case
I am here patiently waiting for a time
not so jading
An emotional mirage placed for
protection
Or maybe for reactive deflection

Vehemence (PCS)

My life is in boxes
And I don't know where my sock is
The way I'm thinking feels a little toxic
And the desperation in my eyes gives away my sadness is on a high
At the drop of a hat I might cry
Deep vehemence heavy and holding
And the way I feel
It's like my chest is exploding
Pacing around the empty house
Feeling the memories as they composite
Leaving some…for a profit
But remembering the footsteps we took
Where we sat with the kids lost in books
The breath you lost
The night the ambulance was called
Leaving this type of grieving feels…

A little releasing

<u>Time travel</u>

Maybe if I leave your clothes
You'll come back…
Maybe if I hug him so tight I'll feel the
remnants you embedded into him
Making this situation less grim
I wish I could go back to 1989
So I could see you again for the first
time
But time travel isn't real
And memories are losing their feel
8 months is too long
The scent of you has long gone…

Still
How I wish time travel was real

Kinetoscope

A fractured wave that projects your voice
Running into my ears and drowning with white noise

And by the way

It's always an almost touch that I can feel
Dreams on a kinetoscope show you like a silent reel
Standing with my arms out

It's still your touch that I can never feel

Your foot steps are the dominant sound
Playing on the phonograph
Round and round

One after the other

Heavy and loud
On the hollow wood floors
Rotting now

And truth be told
There are no flowers to behold
While pledged to be filled
There's only promises left to wilt

FEAST

Gathering around for a feast
My thoughts are consuming all of my peace
Weeping with the willow that I lie beneath
Till dawn breaks through
So quietly

Sunny Clouds

Now etched upon my skin colors of a variety
And daylights gloom is traumatically tantalizing

While I could say the sun is my friend
The dramatic clouds pull me in

I'm a walking contradiction

Lastly
No pressure from the grey to run and hide
The sun pelts the rays leaving me raspberry on the outside
And the sunny clouds tan my hide

Minds state

Behold my words of truth
As I lay here feeling the noose
It's getting tighter and tighter as I speak
And I'm starting to feel weak
My voice breaks as I shake
Reason is telling my brains mistake
With sensations I can barely swallow
My throat is closing as I wallow
Sadness isn't a minds state
Sadness is a flood and I'm a gate

62 & 35

62 and where are you?
You're somewhere new

35… still here
With an emptiness between my ears
Figuratively missing
With incoherently significant distance
Pieces scattered here and there
Brown, blonde and grey hair
Drops from eyes
As we cry
I hope turn to warm rain
And you dance in surprise

<u>July</u>

It's your first birthday in the clouds
Are you alone or is there a crowd
Because I know you wish you could
be here
All sitting around outside in those red
chairs
Laughing and cooking
Drinks in hand
As you watch your grandkids frolic in
wonderland

But now I'll let these balloons fly
I hope you catch them in the sky
And make the biggest bouquet
And have the best day
And added to my list
I'll have to explain
Why July 1st is another painful day

Almost

The typing is silent as is your voice in the quiet
I'm begging for a hint of enlightenment
But my fortitude is in solitary confinement
Tangled and reaching through the branches
Worm holes keep taking my almost chances
If I could just find a way
To keep the danger at bay
While my brain is compiling ways to combat it
Maybe this time I could keep it and not almost have it

Satchel

To whom do I owe this debt
This burden I now bear
I plea
Please don't make me carry it all
It's too much
I'll crumble
I'll fall
Yet I gather it back up brick by brick
While being watched by these useless pricks
Why are you here
I scream out bewildered
Sincerity
Should be considered
With my satchel full of recollections
I wallow
In search to find someone to give affection

Imposter syndrome

I'm an imposter in a unified form
As a human
It kind of feels like something to mourn
With a delicate life
Decisions to decide
Imposter syndrome is on high
And it's not the right foot I started on
It's divertedly wrong
You left me
And it felt like an atomic bomb
My world is gone
Who am I
I'm trying to decide
But ignorance is my guide

The end.

Acknowledgements

Thank you, daddy, my husband, my big brother, and cousin Tawny, for pushing me to publish my heart into a book and reading all my poems I sent you while writing them. Thank you to my sister-in-law Tarryn for also reading my poems and being able to tell my mood from them and tell me what I needed to hear in that moment. I'm not sure how you do it but you did. And thank you to Aunt Marie for volunteering to read my manuscript to help me. Thank you to my son Rebel for drawing the pictures for me! One more thanks to everyone else who has supported me on this or really my writing abilities ever. Thank you I love y'all!
I know reading my poems wasn't easy with all the emotions behind them, so I am sincerely grateful for y'all.

Howdy, I'm Kelani! I'm a daughter, sister, wife and a mama to 3 little boys and a beautiful stepdaughter. I like sad songs and tattoos. I'm also terrible at keeping things in order. See what I mean…. I'm the author of this book…if that wasn't obvious and more to come. (I'll try write happier stuff).

I have been writing stories, songs, plays and poetry for as long as I can remember. I'm from the southwest. Oh also, I like my coffee with honey.

Big thank you to Jonathan Mondragon(my husband) for listening and being my illustrator, I love you.

And well, okay that's all for now.

I'm probably working on another book! So please go and find out more at @kkmondragon1 on Instagram and @kelani.mondragon on TikTok

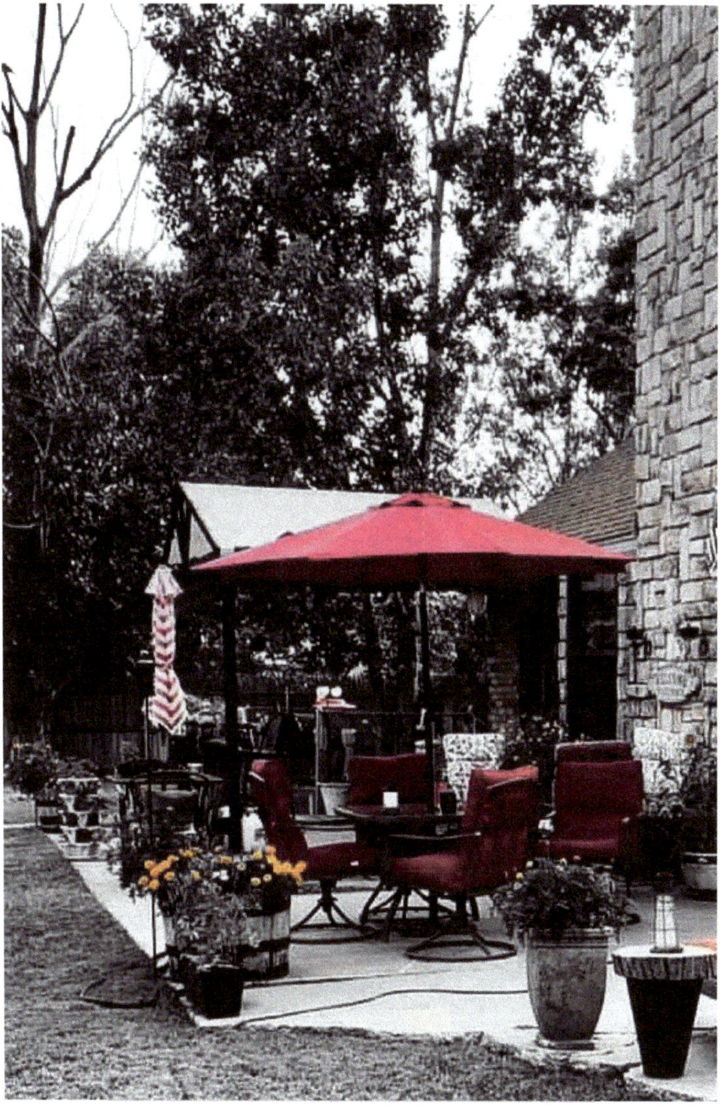

Milton Keynes UK
Ingram Content Group UK Ltd.
UKHW020810141124
451205UK00009B/512